www.avocadobooks.com

First published by Avocado Books in 2017

Text and illustrations copyright © Gill Thomas 2017

ISBN: 978-0-9935658-6-1

Gill Thomas asserts the moral right to be
identified as the author of this work

A catalogue record of this book is
available from the British Library

This book is to record my gratitude to my
husband and parents.

It is dedicated to my sons, grandchildren and
great-grandchildren.

My Fifties London

Gill Emett Thomas

Contents

			Page
Chapter 1	Making a start at art college		9
Chapter 2	Elliott Advertising		17
Chapter 3	Arriving in London		25
Chapter 4	Settling in		33
Chapter 5	Going out with Ray		41
Chapter 6	Mainly clothes		49
Chapter 7	In and around London		57
Chapter 8	Family visits and a new flat		65
Chapter 9	Getting married		73
Chapter 10	Living in Edgware		81
	Aftermath		89

Epstein's Lucifer in the Birmingham Art Gallery

Chapter 1 - Making a start at art college

I was born in Birmingham in 1933. My father, Bill Emett, came from a family with an interest in graphic art. His grandfather had been a court lithographer. One of his cousins was a successful fashion artist in Fleet Street and his brother was a well-known cartoonist of the time; Rowland Emett of Punch magazine. From the earliest age I enjoyed looking at drawings and illustrations of every kind.

In 1949, on leaving school at sixteen, I applied for a place at Birmingham College of Art and Design. For my preliminary interview with the principal, Meredith Hawes, I had to take along samples of my work. These were approved, although I was firmly instructed not to roll up my drawings in future, but to keep them flat in an art folder.

On the appointed day I gathered with the other first year students at the Margaret Street College, near Birmingham Town Hall and the Art Gallery. First we were directed to the college art supplies office and shown where to buy art folders, drawing boards and supplies of paper, pencils and charcoal. Then, rather to our surprise, we were told that most of our first year classes would be spent at an outpost, coming in to the

Birmingham College of Art and Design

main college for history of art lectures or to work in the clay room. This outpost turned out to be part of a rather grim old secondary school in Dudley, a far from impressive venue.

However, glad to be together with fellow students, we all piled on to the bus to Dudley. Here we found the school, traversed a bleak playground, were directed upstairs, and found a large well-lit classroom studio and our tutor for the year, Mr Colley.

At first, from his sardonic demeanour, I think we were rather a trial to Mr Colley. He once referred to our group of young girls as the 'Little Ovaltinies'. At the time a frequently heard radio jingle in praise of Ovaltine was sung on Radio Luxembourg by a group of irritatingly sweet and chirpy young voices!

We were a group of about sixteen school leavers, an equal number of boys and girls. Just one of our number was an older, tall ex-RAF man named Tony. He quickly became a two-some with a more mature American girl. They were both liked by us all.

I remember a dark Welsh boy named Peter Dart and his rather more enigmatic friend Charles Wood. There was a tall sophisticated girl, named Juanita Waterson and, among others, two friendly girls Liz and Judy. We gradually got to know each other, became a cohesive group and began to benefit from our instruction.

In the fifties there was no mention of conceptual art. During our Foundation Year we were given introductory work in a variety of fields; anatomy, life drawing, lettering, stage and costume design, relief printing, 3D work in clay and so on. There was one activity, which embarrassed us all which was called Creative Dance. Just one lovely shy girl enjoyed it as when it came to dancing she was totally unselfconscious, unlike the rest of us.

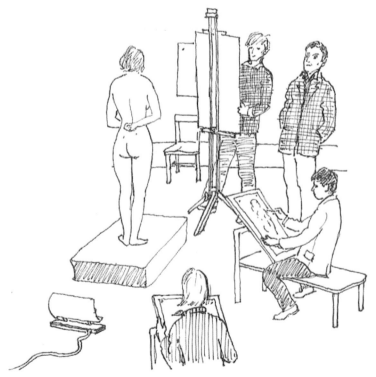

In the main college where we went on Monday evenings for brilliant history of art-illustrated talks by the austere lecturer, we mingled with designers, architects, sculptors and painters. Everyone was learning, honing and developing their skills and then using them to express themselves. As far as I was concerned it was absolute bliss and I enjoyed every minute.

After the restrained atmosphere of my previous rather select all-girls school, this new world offered more exciting and unpredictable possibilities.

During the first year we did a great deal of drawing, particularly life drawing. We had three regular models – Fred an old ex-boxer, Phylis a delicate reserved girl with dark red hair and a cheerful friendly woman who had a young daughter. Learning how the body was constructed and how it moved gave us all more confidence in figure drawing.

Throughout our time at the Dudley outpost we enjoyed going to a lorry drivers' pull-up cafe on the busy main road. It was cheap and cheerful and run by a lively young man named Alec. We would crowd into its steamy warmth for cups of tea and hot buttered toast. There was a jukebox to belt out the latest hits if we had money for the machine. We loved it.

On one occasion we were given individual projects. We could choose any subject matter we liked to be the focus of a series of drawings. I chose to visit Derrit End, a poor part of the city, and draw some of the grimy old buildings linked to Birmingham's industrial past. I remember that one student, a quiet, apparently insignificant boy, produced a series of fluent detailed drawings that amazed us by his remarkable ability. His parents ran a post office and his drawings showed the many transactions that took place. I remember especially a drawing of hands counting out money at speed. It was astonishing in its confidence and accuracy.

Mr Colley was an imaginative teacher and sometimes took us out of college, once taking us to Litchfield Cathedral for the day. My favourite outing, long to be remembered was when we went by coach to Harvington Hall, an old moated manor house in Worcestershire, full of priests' hiding holes as it had been a secret Catholic stronghold at a time of bitter Protestant persecution. It was a cold winter's day with thin snow on the ground. Geese were pecking about beneath the bare trees as we approached.

First we were shown round the building and saw the priests' cleverly concealed hiding holes. One small room, its walls painted with drops of blood and tears between the half-timbering, held a strong emotional charge. After exploring we all settled down in various places to draw in the ancient bare rooms. Unknown to us, Mr Colley must have organised a record player, because as we worked in the silent slightly sinister old building the strains of Tudor music crept through the rooms with eerie effect.

Inspired by this intense experience I rapidly made about six pen and wash drawings in Indian ink, perhaps the most free, confident work I had produced to date. The next day, back in the classroom we were asked to pin up our work for discussion. Mr Colley then sent me off on an errand and apparently then praised my drawings. Perhaps he didn't want me to become complacent! I quickly learned my limitations. When required to produce completely imaginative work or to work in two or three dimensions I was disappointingly inept. It seemed I needed to work from real people or real scenes to produce my best work.

Now, long since, Harvington Hall has been taken over by the National Trust so that the warmer, brighter, beautifully furnished rooms are very different from the austere building we encountered.

As the time passed Mr Colley grew less sardonic and we appreciated his guidance to our mutual satisfaction. Gradually, as we experienced many possible approaches to our future art careers, we began to gravitate towards the fields we preferred. For instance Juanita Waterson excelled in stage and costume design and was determined to work in the theatre. In later years it was quite common to see her name in the costume credits for television dramas. Sometimes we all went to parties together. Most of the students were going to study for their National Diploma of Design qualifications but, because I wanted to make my way in the graphic art world, I was planning to focus on illustration and book design in my second year.

Understanding my interests so well, my father told me that it was likely that to gain entry to a commercial art studio I would have to start at the bottom on a very low wage. He suggested that I began to start applying now and not to wait until the end of the four year Art Course. Professional studios of the time, which he understood from his brother's past experiences, were apt to say, 'We will consider taking you on when you have some experience of the commercial art process'. No one ever explained how you were to acquire that experience.

As a result of this advice, in the Summer break after my Foundation Year, I took a holiday job for six weeks in the studio of a small advertising agency in Broad Street, Elliott Advertising.

As the studio's artists took their annual holidays there were spare desk spaces and here I was given a variety of jobs to do. I only managed to hear of this job because an old school friend of my father's, Bert Blexley, was art director at the agency.

Here at Elliott Advertising I could see the whole advertising process: consultation with clients, rough layouts, finished layouts, finished artwork, lettering and copywriting. There were no technical aids apart from a primitive machine known as the 'dodger' which could enlarge or reduce images to trace. Most of the lettered headings were drawn by hand. Sometimes they were typeset along with copy produced by the agency's copywriters. The adhesive letters of Letraset were sometimes used.

'53

The men working in the studio were all extremely skilled, all specialising in a particular field. I began to be given figurative work as none of the other artists were especially interested in this area. I continually practised different techniques and ideas.

The studio manager allocated jobs to the various artists as the work came in. He was helpful and sympathetic and explained everything clearly to me. All the studio artists were friendly and I enjoyed my time there. I was given a desk facing down the narrow studio and made a sketch of everyone working there one afternoon.

I was hoping I might be taken on there permanently sometime in the future.

After this holiday job I returned to college, finding the second year very different.

For one thing we now studied every day at the main college in Margaret Street. We were assigned lockers on the first floor corridor, which made life easier. In contrast to our outings to Alex's cafe we now had coffee in the college refectory in the basement where we mingled with older artists.

Throughout my art training I had kept in constant touch with my two closest school friends, Jean and Ann. They had both been to secretarial college in central Birmingham during my first year. Now that I was no longer based in Dudley but back in Margaret Street, and they had jobs nearby, we could meet more easily during the week. Sometimes we met for lunch at a Lyons restaurant in the town's main square. We all enjoyed our continuing friendship as our different career paths brought about changes.

The main college at Margaret Street

My second year illustration course was led by two humorous tutors, Mr Palmer and Mr Price, and was useful and interesting. Our original group was now often dispersed as we often studied different subjects, although all of us still continued with our life drawing studies, in the splendid life drawing studios.

Occasionally we were taught there by a tall elderly man, rather frail and self-effacing. He was stooped and wore an ancient suit. He would sometimes demonstrate particular corrections to our work by drawing in the margins of our paper. To our astonishment we saw him effortlessly and brilliantly draw small explanatory sketches which immediately helped us to improve our work. For me he showed exactly how the eye sat in its socket from different angles. We felt awed by such ability and tried to find out more about him. Apparently, when young, he had won the Prix de Rome and had gone to Italy to work for three years. Towards the end of this period all his superlative work had been destroyed in a fire. He then had some form of breakdown. What happened to him in the long time between his youthful brilliance and his appearance in our life drawing studio we had no idea. We warmed to his gentle courtesy and were grateful for the clarity of his instruction.

Now, being in the centre of town, we were close to Birmingham Art Gallery and were encouraged to go there frequently to draw and examine all the different collections. There was a particularly good collection of Pre-Raphaelite painters. They were rather out of fashion at the time but we could all appreciate their masterly use of paint. Something else that fascinated me in the costume collections were some 18th century mens'
waistcoats. The embroidered colours and designs were so varied and exquisite I had rarely seen such beautiful colour combinations. However, my absolutely favourite piece was a bronze statue of Lucifer by Epstein, positioned below a glass dome in the roof of the gallery. Poised lightly on one foot, ready to push off and soar upwards, this figure emanated a powerful force field. I was continually drawn to it. It was the single most exciting work of art I had encountered to date.

As my second year drew to a close I said goodbye to the college, my tutors and friends, and applied for full time work at Elliott Advertising. I was told that there was no vacancy in the studio but that they would employ me doing odd jobs until a vacancy occurred. I was determined to take advantage of the offer.

*This cover was a joint studio effort. I drew the men, another
artist did the motorbikes and another the lettering.*

Chapter 2 - Elliott Advertising

Elliott Advertising could not have been more different from Art College.

Their rather cramped premises were situated above a car showroom in Broad Street, a short bus ride from the city centre. About eight or nine artists were employed. There were several men who handled clients' accounts or who worked in the copy writing department, the managing director and his secretary and several girl typists.

The agency had quite a few clients, including BSA motorcycles, and was permanently busy.

Instead of working in the light-filled studio as I had done on my holiday job I was in an inner room with no direct daylight so that overhead lights were on permanently. Mr Tedstone, a kind fatherly man was my immediate boss for the time being. He was almost constantly on the phone talking to clients and printers.

My job consisted of sticking up-to-date cuttings of every advertisement produced by the agency into large guard books to make a permanent record. This involved combing through all the trade magazines and newspapers where the agency's work was published.

To make this painfully boring work more bearable I kept cuttings books of my own where I collected and cut-out particularly attractive, striking advertisements from other sources. Some of the young layout artists in the studio began to borrow these as inspiration for their own designs.

Occasionally I was sent as a messenger to different offices or factories and, on several occasions, was sent to collect the firm's wages from a bank in the centre of town, travelling by bus. Looking back I think it was a wonder that I was not mugged. Perhaps this occurred to my employers as that particular job ceased. To say that I was naive would be an understatement.

Although the filing job was so drab after the excitement and stimulus of art college, I never for a moment doubted that this was a necessary step towards the career I wanted.

One thing which alleviated the boredom was meeting my friends Jean and Ann in town for lunch. We had an hour for our lunch break. The bus journey in and out of town was about ten minutes each way giving us forty minutes to meet. We went to a rather smart little buttery downstairs at Rowans store, and thoroughly enjoyed catching up with our news.

Ann, Jean and I went to concerts at Birmingham Town Hall

The three of us also spent time together at the weekends, frequently going to the theatre. We liked the Birmingham Rep and often went to Stratford to the Shakespeare Memorial Theatre. I was keen on the young actor Paul Scofield who had several Shakespeare seasons there at this time. Sometimes we would go to the stage door for autographs.

Jean particularly enjoyed music so we also went to concerts at Birmingham town hall, usually conducted by George Weldon. Ann wanted to be an actress at this time and had parts in a small local amateur theatre. Jean and I sometimes went to dances together.

At last, after about six months of this mind-numbing filing work, one of the young artists in the studio left to do his National Service in the army. Immediately I asked Mr Carney-Smith if I could have his free desk and then moved into the studio that day. I was to be paid thirty shillings a week ... I was on my way.

The artists were not used to having a girl permanently in the studio and at first teased me a good deal. I liked them and learned a good deal from watching them work.

Some specialised in hand-drawn lettering, others did layouts or finished artwork. One red-haired Irishman was particularly good at motor-bikes or cars. Even in an alcoholic daze after lunch he could still turn out superb technical drawings.

There were one or two young boys doing menial tasks and learning the ropes from the bottom up.

I enjoyed the atmosphere of the busy cheerful studio, with its big windows looking across the road to old-fashioned terraced houses and shops.

At Elliott's I saw that the priorities for our artwork were very different from those at art college where originality had been prized.

Here, presentation was all. Finished artwork for clients must be immaculate – neatly mounted and protected by crisp clean overlays. Speed of execution was required. Different sorts of tools were used: airbrushes for smooth finish, different types of ruling pens, rulers, set squares and compasses. I learned to use the lethally sharp cutter for trimming card and paper, and the careful technique for mounting work using Cow Gum.

Most of the work I did was figurative. The two years of life drawing at college had given me confidence. None of the other artists were particularly interested in this field so I had many opportunities. Basic metal printing blocks reproduced our work in black and white. Mechanical tints were used for various tones.

I looked at all the magazines I could get my hands on, looking for illustrations I admired. Everyone thought highly of Norman Rockwell who did front covers for the American Saturday Evening Post. I liked the elegant fashion drawings by Eric for Vogue magazine.

Francis Marshall was a very popular illustrator for advertisements and story illustrations. His output was prodigious as everywhere I looked I saw his work. His drawings were quite stylised but lively, looking as though they were dashed off confidently.

I used poster colours to paint from photographic references.

If I had spare time between jobs I used photographic references to paint coloured illustrations or make monochrome drawings. We used small pots of opaque poster colours, which could be diluted to give a colour wash. This was a way of showing the studio manager what I could do. After this I was pleased to be given two front covers for the magazine Motor Cycle Weekly, one in full colour, one in tone. It was exciting to see my work in print.

Most of the top illustrators seemed to work in London, which was where I hoped to go. It was the Mecca of graphic artists at that time. I began to look for jobs in London. I applied to a London agency and received a kindly but dismissive reply. I regularly bought Advertisers Weekly looking for openings. I applied for a small illustrating job on Vogue magazine. I was offered two guineas a week salary. My father could not afford to support me so the job had to be turned down. It sounded as though the other young girls on the magazine appeared to be fairly wealthy 'debs' supported by their fathers. As I carried on with my illustrative work I determined to keep trying for a London opening.

Sometimes the agency's clients came in to the studio to discuss their ideas with the studio manager or the artists themselves. One sophisticated client, a tall, good-looking, immaculately dressed man was the owner of a funeral parlour. He seemed rather amused and wanted to talk to me about designing a reception area for visitors to his offices. During our discussion I asked if he had a particular idea for the colouring of the fitted carpet. 'Oh make it maroon darling,' he said airily, 'the colour of congealed blood!'

On another occasion the man who was the script writer for 'The Archers' radio programme came in. This new daily serial was extremely popular at the time. He was a friendly pleasant man and for some reason he seemed to have connections to the publicity for a company that sold tinned fruit. I was asked to design and illustrate a coloured booklet for children to read about these products.

My work by now was very varied. I still saw my friends Jean and Ann frequently. I joined a small local tennis club. Ann was making applications now to become an air hostess and took a job working in a hotel in Stratford to gain experience for her CV. Jean and I enjoyed a week's package holiday in Paris.

During my third year Elliott Advertising moved from Broad Street to larger premises in Manton House not far from Snow Hill Station. The studio was much larger but gloomier than our previous one. Its windows overlooked industrial chimneys belching smoke. I was

Studio view Manton House, Birmingham

more determined than ever to get to London.

I had got to know some of the younger artists quite well. I went to the cinema with one, skating with another. We all went to a party given by one of the young typists. I didn't have a boyfriend, just boys who were friends.

The first Friday that I did not buy Advertisers Weekly, feeling that there were never any suitable jobs, an interesting advert appeared. Pete, a lively young man from the copy writing department brought the magazine up to the studio to show me. The advertisement invited people to apply to WOMAN magazine to produce general illustrations mainly in black and white. They were asked to send samples of their work to Odhams Press, High Holborn, London. That weekend I sent off my art folder with a range of work, large and small, black and white and full colour.

I then waited in a fever of impatience for a reply. A fortnight later on a Saturday morning I went to collect our weekly joint from the butcher and, on returning home, found that my mother had just taken in a large parcel for me from the postman. Recognising the wrapped shape of my art folder I rushed into the kitchen to open it. There was an official looking letter asking me to come up to London for an interview. We were all excited and tried not to get too hopeful.

My father drove me up to London and sat in on the interview – a circumstance which must sound hilarious to contemporary girls. Odhams Press was housed in a large building next to Holborn Town Hall, and we were shown in to meet 'Tiny' Watts the art editor of WOMAN, a large humorous man who made us welcome. After some discussion he offered me the minimum National Union of Journalist's salary – nine guineas a week. My father and I struggled for neutral expressions of acceptance but were elated. The men in the studio in Birmingham were supporting their families on five guineas a week.

Once our interview was over and we were out on the landing at the head of the stairs we leapt about silently for a minute or two with triumphant relief.

We then made our way to a well-known nearby restaurant called D'ebry's and had a celebratory tea with their famous chocolate cake before driving home with the exciting news to my mother.

I gave in my notice at Elliott Advertising, thanking Pete so gratefully for drawing my attention to the job in Advertisers Weekly and thanking my father's friend Mr Blexley for giving me a start. Now everything began to move quickly

My father contacted his cousin Kathleen whose daughter Sally was studying to be an occupational therapist in St John's Wood in London and it was fixed that I should stay at the same hostel as Sally.

I shared a final happy time with Jean and Ann around the time of my 21st birthday before my parents and I set off for a week's holiday in London. We had a lovely time but as the week progressed I sometimes felt pangs as I saw the time growing ever nearer when they would go home, and I would stay behind.

On my last evening at the hotel when I had gone to bed I told myself that I had made such a song and dance about getting to London that I would now have to get on with it! We all managed to hug and say goodbye cheerfully the next morning when they delivered me to the hostel.

My mother and father had always been supportive and helpful despite the fact that, in those days, not many parents encouraged their girls to go to live and work in London on their own. Quite a few fathers would not even support their daughters going to art college locally and persuaded them to take on secretarial work. It's true that it was hard for young girls to find well-paid graphic art jobs at that time so I was excited to have this opportunity, and grateful to my parents for not putting objections in my way.

Some of the houses were still suffering from bomb damage

Chapter 3 - Arriving in London

The hostel in St John's Wood was run to accommodate girls who were training to be Occupational Therapists at a nearby centre. It consisted of two elegant old houses joined together. The rooms were high ceilinged with attractive proportions. The stairs had beautiful curving banisters.

As with all the similar houses nearby it was shabby. Some of the other houses were suffering from bomb damage not yet repaired. When the tube trains passed below the house trembled gently.

My parents had driven me to St John's Wood on the Saturday morning. Mrs Le Marchand, who ran the hostel, explained to me that the other girls would turn up over the weekend, all being there for Monday morning. She showed me to my room, which looked out over the front door where there were two neat beds. I chose the one nearest the sunny window.

It was lonely in the almost empty old house. From my previous experience of starting boarding school I knew that in a day or two I would feel more at home. After unpacking I found my current book. I had brought along Jane Eyre, an old favourite, and spent some hours reading it. Jane's acute unhappiness at the beginning of this book did little to lighten my mood. Then Mrs Le Marchand introduced me to the girl who was to share my room. She turned up just before lunch time. Not being a new girl she knew the hostel and its routines. She was a South African, friendly and plump. She showed me how to travel the route to the kitchen in the adjoining house where meals were served.

On the Sunday morning when the hostel was still almost empty we went together to London Zoo which was nearby. It was not open to the general public at this time on Sunday mornings but my new friend, Jill, had special tickets obtained by her parents who it appeared were well-to-do and well connected.

By Sunday evening all the girls had arrived and I saw my second cousin Sally. I was pleased to see her, but as she shared a room with a particular friend on another floor of the old house we didn't see much of each other. I looked forward to Monday when I would start at Odhams.

The next morning I travelled down Baker Street and then to High Holborn on the bus. I had been told at my interview that our working day started at ten o'clock. After the much earlier start in Birmingham this seemed quite luxurious.

At 'Woman' offices everyone was welcoming. My immediate boss was Tiny Watts, the Art Editor. He had an office with a corner window looking towards the top of Drury Lane. Tiny introduced me to Pat McNeil and asked her to show me around. Pat was a tall dark attractive girl who designed many of the magazine's page layouts.

On that first morning she took me up to the fourth floor where the general Art Department was set out.

There was a studio manager and quite a large number of men of all ages working upstairs in this general art department. As Pat took me round I saw my future husband for the first time. I saw a dark haired young man absorbed in mounting some work on the top of a plan chest, with rolled up shirt sleeves. He seemed lively and competent and I liked the look of him. He broke off from his work to be introduced as Ray Thomas, gave a grin and said 'Where have you been all my life?' before carrying on with his task. Rather primly I carried on but was secretly pleased by this ridiculous remark.

* * * * *

I was given a desk downstairs beside Pat in the room next to Tiny's office and enjoyed the simple illustrations I was asked to do. At this early stage I was mainly

drawing small decorative borders for written work. I was shown where to get sandwiches nearby and enjoyed the tea lady coming round with her trolley in the afternoon.

Tiny was gregarious, jovial and amusing. He had the lugubrious flexible face of a comedian. I discovered that every day he went out for a long lunch and drank quite heavily. This seemed not to affect his ability to do his job and, as with many journalists of the day, was par for the course.

Different magazines published by Odhams, together with their staff, were housed on different floors of the building. It was a large organisation but with a comfortable friendly atmosphere. I was very glad to be there.

It was the evenings and the weekends that I found harder to cope with as then I still felt quite lonely. The other girls in the hostel were friendly and we sometimes spent time together, but I was really still the outsider at this stage as they all trained together and knew each other from previous terms. I had determined not to go home for at least five weeks as that would encourage me to settle down in London first.

So I began to organise my time. One thing I was determined to do was to draw London scenes. On Saturday I took my small folding stool, drawing pens, ink and drawing pad to the centre of town. Walking up to the top of Burlington Arcade in Piccadilly I turned right and came across the entrance to the Albany, a perfect place to sketch. Sitting down to draw in a corner beside some railings I became absorbed. It was a lovely summer morning and quiet in the little street. Two elegant old ladies tottered past arm in arm talking quite loudly as they were deaf. One said to the other 'You'll never guess what I sell in the ladies' store now Muriel – I'm a specialist in nuns underwear!' Muriel and I were equally surprised.

Back at the hostel I had to get to grips with doing my own washing by hand in an old stone sink in the gloomy basement where there were also drying racks. Once, as I was finishing ironing one of my shirts, the elderly odd job man, Grant, was passing by. He told me he would show me how to fold a freshly ironed shirt so that it could be laid in a drawer with minimum creasing. He did, and I have used this skill for the rest of my life and am still grateful for his demonstration.

I began to sketch London scenes

On another occasion I looked out the phone number of Margaret, a friend from Birmingham days who now lived in London. She and her boyfriend met me and took me rowing on a lake in a London park. It was kind and generous of them to give up their time together and we had a good day. Finally I contacted Daphne, a girl Jean and I had met on our Paris holiday. She lived in London and we had exchanged our details before we left France. We arranged to meet at Oxford Circus the next Sunday afternoon. We would have tea and then she was to take me to a concert afterwards, near the houses of Parliament.

Daphne was over an hour late for our appointment. In the days before mobile phones I couldn't contact her and had no idea whether to wait or to leave. Perhaps I had got the wrong meeting place? It was a hot windy day. I felt very conspicuous and upset. Young girls did not wait about alone on street corners in those days, especially in London. For a time I moved nearer to the BBC where there was a cab drivers shelter and I was so desperate to sit down. Sometime later when I was back at my corner Daphne turned up, to my intense relief. She didn't seem bothered by her late arrival and I was so grateful to see her I didn't want to be angry or to complain. She was never late again for any of our other outings. We met regularly for a while on Wednesdays after work, going to the new Salad Bar in Kingsway for delicious meals and long chats.

When some time later I caught a flu like cold Mrs Le Marchand phoned Odhams for me to say I would not be in for a day or two. Later that morning I was told I had visitors and Tiny and Grahame the fashion editor were shown into my bedroom. They had come to the hostel to see how I was which was very kind and unexpected. Tiny knew that I was living in a hostel away from home and had apparently been concerned. I was astonished – I hope I showed my gratitude. I felt rather embarrassed at the time.

Odhams took a paternalistic attitude to its employers. I later found this sprang from a tradition encouraged by Lord Southwood the head of the publishing house who had died in 1946 He was remembered with affection by many older staff members. Throughout his life he had looked with sympathy on his fellow workers. He was a self-made man with legendary organisational skills who had built Odhams from a small concern into a publishing giant, and was still remembered for his many acts of kindness to his staff.

I benefitted from this caring precedent and realised how unusual it was.

The Summer Term was nearing its end for the occupational therapists and was celebrated by a dance at the hostel.

The walled garden was at its best – a small marquee was set up there with chairs and tables and refreshments. Our lovely sitting room up steps from the garden, had been cleared. With its polished wooden floor it made a small ballroom. Various boyfriends and brothers turned up. A small group of sophisticated people also arrived – perhaps they gate-crashed as no one seemed to know them. There was a blond young man, an older rather effete man and a dramatic girl with long black hair and striking clothes. The dark girl was flirting with the older man and this left the blond boy at rather a loose end, which turned out to my advantage. He was very charming and we had several dances together. It turned out that he was married to the dark girl and they had had a row. Despite this information I enjoyed dancing during that lovely summer evening with such a glamorous partner and felt that coming to London had been a very good move indeed.

By now the first five weeks were up and it was time to go home for the weekend so I packed my small suitcase and eagerly caught the train to Birmingham on the Friday evening. It was lovely to see my parents again and to be welcomed so warmly. We all enjoyed catching up on our news. As the weekend progressed I realised I was longing to get back to London but didn't mention this for fear of hurting my parents.

It was rather ironic to arrive back at the hostel early on the Sunday evening to find everybody out and the building as lonely and deserted as on my first arrival. However, soon everyone turned up from their weekend activities and things returned to normal.

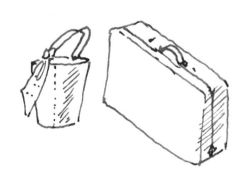

It was only many years later when my sons went off to university and college that I understood how hard it must have been for my parents to see their only child go off without a backward glance.

While it is a cause of very great satisfaction to see one's children leave home to embrace a new future with confidence, it can call for considerable adjustment for those left behind, I did not really appreciate this at the time.

Standing on the steps of the St John's Wood hostel

Covent Garden

Chapter 4 – Settling in

As it was now the Summer Break for the occupational therapists the hostel emptied once more. A group of foreign girls came to stay for several weeks. They were attending English language schools nearby.

By now I had moved into a larger room at the back, overlooking the garden, which I shared with two new friends, Jane and Anna. Because they were away I was asked to share the room with two French girls. I wasn't happy with the fact that they smoked in bed and never wanted the window open. Fortunately we didn't have to see much of each other. One day they complained to me that they found London dull and not as they had expected.

I felt very indignant. I told them that on the next Saturday I would take them out. Without spending much money I was determined to show them the London I loved.

First I took them to Fortnum & Masons in Piccadilly, to have coffee. All their criticisms died away in the face of the undoubted glamour and sophistication of our setting and its affluent clientele.

After some window shopping we went to the Soup Kitchen behind the Coliseum for lunch. Here simple meals of soup, crusty bread and cheese were served. It was inexpensive but trendy and attractive.

Finally I took them to the luxurious cinema in Curzon Street to see a much publicised film. After this I heard no more complaints. In fairness to the French girls they had only seen the shabby hostel and the streets where their language school was based so I suppose their complaints were fair enough. We got on better after this excursion.

During this time I was getting to know the staff on WOMAN and finding my way around at Odhams. Because I shared a room with Pat McNeil I got to know her first. Previously she had worked in France on Elle magazine and was in her late twenties to my twenty one. She was a good layout artist and designed many of the magazines pages. During the time I knew her she had a succession of boyfriends and appeared worldly-wise to my inexperienced eyes. As with all the other girls and women I met on WOMAN she was friendly and helpful. Because of the rather laid back attitude to time-keeping on the magazine we both occasionally became rather casual about our starting time each day. Tiny Watts hit on a perfect solution to this. He told Pat that he had noticed that I was a bit vague about my timekeeping and asked her to remind me and keep an eye on me.

Without reprimanding either of us he had ensured that both of us would be more exact in future. Clever Tiny!

As our room was an ante-chamber to Tiny's larger room, a succession of illustrators and photographers would pass through. There was one particular Scandinavian illustrator whose work I noticed was extremely well paid. He illustrated quite a number of the love stories, which featured in every number. I realised that successful graphic artists could do very well for themselves.

Occasionally in the afternoon, if Tiny was not occupied, he would come in to see Pat and I. Once, before coming in to our room he put a number of elastic bands round his head so that his face appeared to be scored with the scars of deep razor cuts! Our horror amused him greatly.

On another occasion, at a time when a popular science fiction film was portraying a man with limbs that became distorted and alien, he pushed several old washing up mops up his sleeve and came to look at Pat's work. The hand he rested on her desk appeared to have changed into grey tendrils, provoking screams from us both! These childish pranks endeared him to us.

* * * * *

Before the occupational therapists came back, and there were still some empty beds in the hostel, Jean was able to come and stay one weekend. We did something I

had wanted to do for ages. We got up very early in the dark on the Saturday morning and travelled down to Covent Garden flower market on the tube. Here, in the cool echoing market, everything was bustling and busy. The fresh delicate smell of the flowers was overwhelming. Their massed ranks of colour and fragrance made it well worth the effort of getting up so early. We revived our flagging energy with a hot breakfast of eggs, bacon and sausages at a small cafe in the market. We thoroughly enjoyed catching up on our news during the weekend.

* * * * *

My father knew of my interest in the work of Francis Marshall, the fashion artist and illustrator, as I had collected many of his drawings before I left home. Seeing an article about him in the paper and realising he lived beside Primrose Hill, not too far from my St

John's Wood hostel, he wrote to him asking if he had any advice for his daughter just starting her career. As a result of this correspondence Francis Marshall invited me round to tea at his beautiful house. He also invited another girl with similar interests, which we both felt was extremely good of him. The other girl was called Violet and we were rather over-awed and shy. He turned out to be an elegant quiet man but it was his wife that was the real surprise. All the women in his illustrations had a particular way of walking, standing or sitting, a particular tilt of the head. His cool slim wife looked exactly like these illustrations and I realised he had not invented this sophisticated type of woman as I had supposed, but had used his wife as the model for much of his work.

He suggested that Violet and I should go to St John's Wood Art Club to do life drawing and told us he would speak to the committee to set up these visits. Apparently a supper was provided at these evening classes and was included in the weekly cost.

Illustration to the
Stork Club, New York
by
Francis Marshall

The next week Violet and I went along together to the art club. This turned out to be a rather old fashioned dark building where access was gained through a shrubbery.

The whole experience was rather a shock to us. First of all we sat down with a group of middle aged and elderly men for a very good meal in a formal dining room where we were waited upon. While the men were not exactly hostile to us I don't think they were pleased to receive us into their entirely masculine company.

I was slightly startled by a very large erotic painting of 'Leda and the Swan' above the dining room sideboard. When, after the meal, we went through into the warm panelled life drawing room I was pleased to find a very good female model and felt more confident when we started to draw. The model had a luscious figure and was very professional. I was pleased with the drawings I made.

Magazines of the fifties

After a few weeks attending this art club both Violet and I felt that we were definitely intruding into these rather self-indulgent private gatherings and ceased our visits. I wondered it there had been a mischievous element in Francis Marshall's suggestion to us to go there – or perhaps he was just pleased to point us in the right direction for some life drawing with excellent models close to where we both lived. At our tea party he had told us that he himself had been to the club but had stopped going after some time.

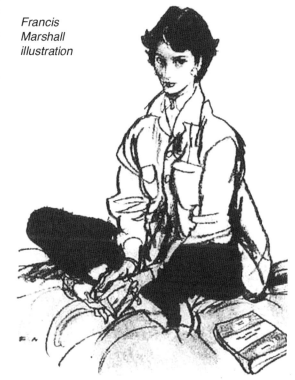

Francis Marshall illustration

* * * * *

Gradually I was discovering more about other members of WOMAN staff.

The most important person was the editor, Mary Grieve. Because WOMAN had huge circulation figures she was treated with respect in the magazine publishing world. In the days before television took off cheap popular magazines were very influential with large advertising revenues. Mary Grieve was a cool authoritative figure and was rarely seen. She was chauffeur driven in from the country each day. A tall, dark-haired, laconic American woman nicknamed 'Higg' was Mary Grieve's assistant. She was well liked by all of us. I suppose both these women would have been in their fifties.

Archie Kay was responsible for the financial management of the magazine and was often seen about.

Mary Davis was the fashion editor, a small dark intense woman with an upper-class manner. I later learned that she was profoundly deaf and that Grahame Hall, her personal assistant, worked very closely with her. Together they made an effective team.

I met Betsy Lamb, daughter of the writer and journalist Rita Lamb, and Margaret Smith who researched and wrote about beauty products. Evelyn Home, the problem page editor, and Ruth Morgan, the cookery editor, were among the weekly contributors to the magazine.

Although most of the women who worked on the magazine had interesting well paid careers and wide opportunities it was always assumed that our readers lived more conventional lives. All the writers of the articles subscribed to the idea that their readers were housewives and that if they did have jobs they were all aspiring to marriage and motherhood. The articles on fashion, cookery, home furnishings, beauty, knitting, dressmaking and so on conjured up a mythical world of happy girlfriends, and contented housewives and mothers with pleasant manly boyfriends and husbands hovering in the background. A high moral tone was taken for granted. Gender roles were clearly defined. Issues of class, politics, educational opportunities and personal ambition were never mentioned.

The tone of the magazine was always positive and cheerful. It was full of information of a practical nature and was generally acknowledged to be reliable, for example the recipes always worked and were easy to follow.

A dress pattern illustration

It must have answered a need as proved by the large circulation figures. It had a popular rival named WOMAN'S OWN published by Newnes which was slightly more adventurous stylish and racy. Our circulation figures generally topped theirs to our satisfaction. Both magazines were in every hairdressers in the land and many thousands of homes. Even people who professed to despise these magazines, preferring something more up-market, would sometimes be seen flicking through them. Their advertising revenue must have been phenomenal for their time.

We felt lucky to have good jobs with friendly staff and colleagues and liked having access to all the opportunities London had to offer right on the doorstep.

I enjoyed my job. Starting with small illustrations for written pieces I gradually progressed to more ambitious and varied work. Occasionally I was sent out to sketch and bring back details of garments to be featured in the magazine, clothes which could be made up from patterns.

Sometimes I would venture into a full page spread illustrating interior design or furnishing ideas. In the fifties many magazines, papers and advertisements were illustrated by drawings giving hundreds of illustrators opportunities to earn a good living. By great good fortune I had arrived in London at a time when artists were needed and opportunities abounded. It was only some years later that photographs rather than drawings were used to illustrate many articles and drawn illustrations suffered something of a decline.

* * * * *

I continued to draw London scenes

The Grenadier, Belgravia

Chapter 5 – Going out with Ray

By now I had become friendly with two girls who occupied a small room next to the fashion department. They both did secretarial work. Pam was about my age, Jane somewhat older. We quite often went out to lunch together.

Sometimes clothes or artefacts for photographic sessions would pass through their room. One day someone left a little glass Buddha on the corner of Pam's desk. She and I were there alone. Picking it up we chatted about it and hoped it would have a benign effect on their office.

Pam knew I was hoping to get to know Ray better and I knew she was interested in Brian, a young man working on another magazine in the Odhams building.

Suddenly, quite spontaneously, we decided to ask the little Buddha for help. We placed it on top of the tall cupboard in the corner of the room. Then, standing before it, part seriously and partly as a joke, we made our requests. I said I would like to go out with Ray. Pam said she would like to go out with Brian. Then quickly, before anyone else came into the room, we took down the Buddha and hurried away.

Somehow this symbolic making of requests gave each of us the impetus to further our plans.

The next time I stopped to chat with Ray in the general art department I told him I was trying to find out about evening classes for life drawing, and asked if he knew of any locally. He told me he went to St Martins nearby and was going to enrol the next Thursday for the coming term and asked if I would like to come along.

Overjoyed I sped downstairs to tell Pam. She had spoken to Brian when she met him on the stairs outside her office and found herself agreeing to go out with him. We were both delighted but rather awed by the success of our efforts.

On the following Thursday Ray took me to St Martins and we both enrolled, and then went to the life drawing room. The model was excellent and I thoroughly enjoyed making drawings on crisp cartridge paper with sanguine crayon. It was good going with Ray and we went for several weeks. Before this Ray had only seen the illustrations I had done for Woman magazine. Now, seeing that I was a confident artist, he asked if I would do a painting for him. He was redecorating his room at home and wanted a painting for the main wall.

I was pleased to be asked and made sketches of a scene in Chelsea in the dusk. I had brought my oil paints with me from home so just needed somewhere to begin work. I asked if I could use a room in the hostel which was used as a classroom during the week but was unoccupied during the weekend. Then, over the next couple of weekends, I made the oil painting. I kept the finished painting in our hostel bedroom while it gradually dried out.

Sometime while the painting was in my room Mrs Le Marchand saw it and liked it. She showed it to Edgar, a middle-aged foreign gentleman who we all took to be her boyfriend. Next time he visited she called me into her office and, during our conversation, he said that as I was obviously a keen artist he would be pleased to talk to me sometime about my future progress. Mrs Le Marchand told me she would let me know when he was free. He seemed to be a clever, cultured man.

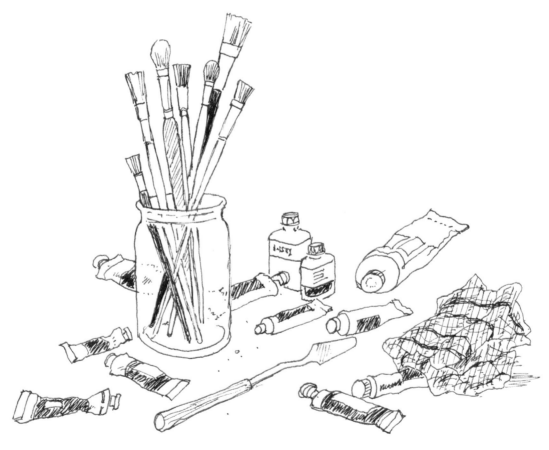

I was pleased about this and mentioned it to my parents when writing home and to Ray when I next saw him. I was rather annoyed when they all humorously warned me to be careful.

Hearing from Mrs Le Marchand that Edgar was free on Saturday afternoon a week or so later, I set off for his flat at Swiss Cottage on the appointed day. When I rang the doorbell an elderly maid let me in and gave me a look of such dislike and disapproval that I was rather taken aback. Thinking that she must be having an off-day I blithely went in to talk to Edgar. He led me in to a small panelled room and sat down opposite me. After some time he said, gesturing towards a chaise long in the corner 'Lie down if you like'. Lie down, I thought, why on earth would I want to want to lie down at 3.30 in the afternoon?

Edgar's conversation now became extremely suggestive and he appeared annoyed at my lack of response. I began to feel very uncomfortable. He suddenly asked testily 'Why exactly did you come here?' Astonished I replied indignantly 'To talk about art!' Not long afterwards I found myself outside walking back to the hostel admitting to myself rather crossly that Ray and my parents had been right all along.

Meanwhile Ray's picture was now dry enough to move and I gave it to him. He seemed very pleased with it and asked me how much he owed me. 'Oh' I said 'I don't want any money for it.' 'Well in that case,' he said 'I'll take you out – where would you like to go?'

SALAD DAYS

At the time everyone was talking about a new musical called Salad Days, which had first been seen in Bristol and had just now transferred to the West End so I asked to go to that. It was lively and fun with catchy lyrics and music. Whether it was really good or not I hardly noticed – I was so happy to be out with Ray. From then on we went out regularly together.

We went to films, concerts and the theatre. Sometimes we ate lunch together at a little Greek restaurant a few minutes' walk from Odhams.

After a time we developed a favourite routine for evenings out. After work we would walk into Soho and on the corner of Soho Square visit MokaRis, one of the first coffee bars in London. Here we had coffee made by a loud hissing coffee machine, and ate one of the specialities on offer. Other young couples would be starting their evenings out together, all of us enjoying ourselves. Then we would walk to the Coach and Horses in Mayfair or go to the Grenadier pub in a mews in Belgravia. Here we could spend the rest of the evening sitting in these comfortable surroundings talking together and really getting to know each other.

I discovered that Ray was 24, three years older than me. He seemed much older in some ways because he had been working since he was 14, had fought in Korea and knew London very well. He also seemed to have had many girlfriends. I found it exciting to be going out with him. He told me much later that he found to his pleasant surprise

that I was really interested in him as an individual which apparently was very different from the flirtatious attentions he usually received form his previous good time girlfriends.

The Grenadier was the perfect place for us to be together. In the early evening it was usually quiet. Among a few others a couple of middle aged WVS ladies were often there too, enjoying a drink and supper together. The rooms were small and intimate. There was always a fire if the weather was cool. One older barman had the mellifluous easily recognised tones of a well-known previous BBC newsreader and announcer. It was one of our favourite haunts, where we were not likely to be disturbed or interrupted.

Ray's grandparents and parents were Londoners and he had been born in the East End. When he was four years old his family had moved to the village of Ewell near Epsom in Surrey. His father and older brother were both printers and worked at Odhams Press in Long Acre, London.

I told him that, although I had been born in Birmingham, three of my grandparents had all lived in London prior to moving to Birmingham. I had heard tales of London all my life and in my late teens my parents and I had made holiday visits here so that parts of London were familiar to me. I felt at home here.

Ray had always wanted to be an artist and had been to Epsom Art College for a while, before starting work as a messenger boy in Fleet Street. Like me he had gained invaluable experience later, working in the studio of an advertising agency, before coming to Odhams to work in the general art department.

Drawing of Fleet Street by Francis Marshall

Barbara Goalen
© John French/Victoria and Albert Museum, London

Chapter 6 – Mainly clothes

The fashions of the early fifties were glamorous but essentially quite staid. The famous top models were often elegant mature women. Hats, pearls and gloves were much in evidence and the one feature they all possessed was an extremely small waist. Each woman's final appearance was a formidable 'production' – reliant on expensive foundation garments, carefully fitted clothes, well-chosen accessories, elaborate jewellery and make-up.

This was before the days of Twiggy and Mary Quant and the leggy young girls of Carnaby Street and the Kings Road. The cult of extreme youth had not begun.

Barbara Goalen was typical of the elegant models continually featured in the press. Tall, beautifully presented and groomed, her haughty features were frequently photographed by John French, one of London's top fashion photographers. His work appeared in virtually every newspaper and magazine throughout the land.

I found it surprising that he also photographed fashion shots for WOMAN magazine. He was obviously adaptable and clever to come to terms with the fact that our requirements would be very different; the last thing we would set out to promote was elegance. Our models were required to be pretty and pleasing and, above all, to appear happy and good natured. This was the type of woman the magazine promoted. Their clothes were designed to be practical and attractive, not expensive or exclusive.

I remember Mary Davis and Grahame Hall talking about John French with great admiration on returning from various fashion shoots with him. He was generally admired and appreciated in London at that time.

WOMAN magazine was always sent invitations to all the fashion shows as were the other women's magazines. Because the clothes were too up-market for us and unsuitable for our publication, I was occasionally sent off in a taxi to enjoy them. This Mayfair world of spindly gilt chairs, elaborately dressed and made up models and grimly professional fashion writers was entertaining.

I was once hissed at by a ferocious older woman with an upholstered bosom and pearls because I was sketching. I think she thought I was a spy because no drawings or photographs of the new collection were allowed out into the press without their permission. It was all great fun.

On one occasion in an elegant house in Mayfair I saw the famous dress designer Hardy Amies among the gathering. He came over to talk to me and was very pleasant. I think he was rather surprised to see such an obviously unsophisticated young girl among the very smart crowd and wondered what I was doing there.

As time passed and I became busier with my illustrations at the magazine these forays into the fashion world ceased but I certainly enjoyed them at the time.

Like most of my young contempories at Odhams I usually wore blouses and skirts or dresses which were neat and fresh but otherwise unremarkable in every way. One day, looking in the windows of the French store Gallerie Layfayette in Regent Street, Ray remarked on one of the dresses in the window display, 'That would suit you Gill, you could wear that'. For some reason I was faintly put out by this remark, perhaps taking it for criticism of my unadventurous clothes. Anyway, the following day I returned to the shop, tried on the dress, liked it, bought it, and took it home to the hostel.

I had some idea of how much it changed my appearance by the reaction of my friends. When I told them I had just bought a new dress they said 'try it on and show us'. When I emerged from where I had been changing they were at first speechless with surprise which was gratifying. The dress was fitting, beautifully cut, made of soft fine pinkish cream wool with a roll neckline. I wore it with a gold chain belt. Nothing could have been more different from my usual choice of clothes.

The next Saturday evening when Ray and I were meeting to have a meal in a smart restaurant in Curzon Street I took off my coat to reveal my new dress to Ray's delighted surprise. Ray had an eye for style and very good taste. He was always well dressed himself. In the mid-fifties men still dressed formally for work. He had all his suits made for him by a tailor in Soho.

After returning from fighting in the tragic Korean war where so many of his friends had been killed and not expecting to come back alive, he was determined to make the most of every opportunity that came his way from now on. He worked hard, had prodigious energy and was ambitious. He had had little education, beginning work as an errand boy in Fleet Street at fourteen. In the past this would have held him back. Without a good education opportunities were limited. Now, however, changes were sometimes offering new chances. When he was working as a graphic artist in an advertising studio he quickly made progress. He was able to do a good deal of overtime and earn very good money. He saved for good clothes, went to galleries, exhibitions, films and the theatre.

The French Dress

He read widely. He already had an inherent love of music, and enjoyed and was knowledgeable about music of all kinds. He ate out at a variety of restaurants and knew London very well.

So I benefited from having a boyfriend who, in the terms of the day, was very much a 'man about town'. I admired Ray's energy and enterprise and he seemed pleased by my appreciation while also recognising in me a desire to explore new possibilities too. It was a time of rejuvenation after the privations of the post war years and London was offering excitement and opportunities for us both.

All the people working at Odhams were members of the National Union of Journalists. Ray keenly attended the union meetings so I quite often went with him. I seem to remember that they were held in the lunch hour in a very large packed hall. Sometime later everyone was awarded a Union rise of back pay. Newly arrived I didn't really understand the ramifications of this event but was very pleased to receive the money. I think some people may have been annoyed that I received this money without having negotiated long and hard to get it as they had done. I understood their resentment but was delighted with the result.

Now that I was going out with Ray so regularly, and we were accepted as a couple, I wanted a special dress in case we were able to go to dances together. My mother and I had been to Harvey Nicholls in Knightsbridge when I was a teenager so I was aware of how expensive it would be. Emboldened by my pay rise money I went there one Saturday and found just the dress I wanted. It was plain, made of beautifully cut heavy slipper satin in pale turquoise.

Soon afterwards Jane, one of my room-mates at the hostel, invited Ray and I to her 21st birthday celebrations at St Albans. One of her friends kindly gave us a lift there and back. We had a good time at the smart dinner dance organised for the event and I was grateful to the opportune pay rise for providing a glamorous dress just in time.

Mrs Le Marchand offered to lend me a fur wrap for the long cold car journey. I was very grateful because the wrap was so warm and comfortable. I had grown up seeing my mother and grandmother wearing fur coats and, at the time, this was accepted as normal. Now times have changed so much and our opinions are so different that I would feel uncomfortable wearing real fur.

Diaghilev Exhibition

Soon after this Ray heard about an unusual exhibition to be put on not far from our favourite haunt, The Grenadier in Belgravia. The ballet critic and designer Richard Buckle was taking over a large imposing building called Forbes House to mount an exhibition on Diaghilev the Russian impresario.

One dark evening we found the venue, wondering what to expect.

The whole experience was extraordinary. In the shadowy painted hall, two brooding larger than life figures guarded the imposing staircase. Music and colour emerged from the darkness. My memories of all the treasures in the richly painted rooms are hazy. Various dramatic tableau were set up, one on the stairway. My favourite room housed vivid colourful costume designs for various Russian ballets. We learned that Richard Buckle was a flamboyant character and admired his panache and showmanship.

In the fifties this kind of experience was rare and was never forgotten by either of us.

Freelance magazine illustration

As Christmas approached I learned that Odhams always took large public rooms nearby to accommodate the staff from all their magazines. Here they put on a Christmas party where everyone met for drinks after work.

Here I was introduced to some of Ray's friends from other magazines – writers, graphic artists and photographers. They were all very nice to me but rather surprised to see Ray as part of a couple, as he had long been known for playing the field!

We were both planning to spend time at home with our families for Christmas. After travelling back on the train I told my parents all about Ray. We talked about how they could meet him which pleased us all and we had a happy Christmas together.

One of the high spots of the holiday was a very good time at my cousin Norma's. Her parents, my Uncle Ralph and Aunt Hilda, had organised a lively party. After some energetic party games, and before we had supper, we had a quiet competition. We were shown a number of boards covered with pasted on advertisements. The name of each of the advertised products was cut out and we had to guess the brand of each advert. I was pleased to win this competition and delighted to see among the prizes some Senior Service cigarettes that I could choose and take back for Ray, they were his favourites.

It didn't worry me at the time that Ray smoked because so did the majority of the male adult population. Smoking had been particularly prevalent during the war and afterwards many people carried on. I can't remember any link being made between smoking and ill health.

The practice was made glamourous by films of the day where the stars frequently smoked cigarettes. This was just another way that the fifties differed from our present day more informed behaviour.

I didn't smoke myself because when I was about eight years old a small boy offered me a tube of rolled up paper to smoke. This made me cough so badly, and feel so sick, that it put me off the whole idea for ever! I often feel grateful to that small boy.

Green and Stone art suppliers Chelsea

Chapter 7 – In and around London

*Guilletta Massina
and Anthony Quinn
in La Strada*

Back in London again Ray and I continued going out together at every opportunity.

As teenagers we had both been avid cinema-goers. Under Ray's influence I now began to see more foreign films, often at the Academy Cinema in Oxford Street. Through friends of Rays who worked on a film magazine we were sometimes able to get free tickets for important events.

We went to the premier of Fellini's much discussed La Strada at the luxurious cinema in Curzon Street. We had been told that at the end of the film the stars would appear on the stage. During the short interval before this event I went to the ladies cloakroom. Here I found Guilietta Masina smoking tensely and pacing up and down – on seeing me she left abruptly. Shortly afterwards she appeared on stage to rapturous applause. I had caught just a glimpse of the stress that this public appearance was causing her.

We also enjoyed many American films, including Marlon Brando in the ground breaking On the Waterfront, and watched the emergence of Marilyn Monroe - hardly ever out of the news.

Once Ann and I met up and went to see Sabrina Fair, being great fans of Audrey Hepburn.

Ray and I were also keen theatregoers. We were lucky in that it was a time of theatre greats – Ralph Richardson, Peggy Ashcroft, John Gielgud, Peter Ustinov, the Oliviers and many more. Most of the theatre buildings were in traditional style as was impressive Covent Garden where we went to see ballet and opera. Our absolute favourite was the Haymarket theatre.

The Festival Hall on the South Bank was totally different. In those days, not long after it was built for the Festival of Britain, it seemed audaciously modern. Inside, the large spaces, the gleaming pale wood, the airy design were surprising and impressive. The auditorium, with its cantilevered boxes on each side of the performance space, was dramatic. I still loved the older theatres but enjoyed a variety of concerts here.

Unlike me, Ray was very knowledgeable about music of all kinds. He had been often to Soho to hear Ronnie Scott and other jazz musicians with his friend Derek. He had known Derek since evening classes at Art School. I later met him, visiting him at the old watermill in Ewell where he lived. Ray's other great friend was Tony. They had met when they both worked in advertising – until I turned up they had often gone out together with a variety of girlfriends.

I told Ray about my two particular friends Jean and Ann. Ann was an air hostess at this point and Jean doing secretarial work.

The Royal Festival Hall

Through friends, and my outings with Ray, I visited many different parts of London. When I first arrived, before I got to know Ray, I had visited Battersea, staying in the flat of my friend Jane from WOMAN. For a time she and I went to Pyramid Parties which were a craze at the time.

This involved attending a party by invitation and then giving a party yourself to the people you had met at the first party and so on. Jane and I gave a party at her flat and after that it seemed to require travelling to parties all over London together. Once I went on my own because Jane was not well. However, after Jane and I read in the papers that someone involved with a Pyramid Party had been murdered we gave up the scheme!

Later Ray and I would go out locally from Odhams in High Holborn during our lunch hour. We often walked down nearby Drury Lane where the first Sainsbury's store was located and enjoyed shopping in its narrow spotless premises. On other occasions we would pass Endell Street swimming baths where Ray went regularly, on our way to the delights of the bookshops in the Charing Cross Road. Near to the small Greek restaurant where we often had lunch, was the extraordinary umbrella shop with its elaborate facade and window displays. Or we would turn in the other direction past Holborn Town Hall down Kingsway towards Lincoln's Inn and its law courts, seeing young girls playing netball in the central leafy square. The British Museum with its fabulous treasures was not far away.

We often visited or walked through Soho where there were intriguing foreign food shops with enticing smells and unfamiliar foods. Ray showed me an impressive shop selling every kind of kitchenware run by the famous Madame Cadet. He also led me up narrow creaking stairs to meet his tailor. We ate in several small Italian or French Soho restaurants.

Nearby Covent Garden fruit and vegetable market was always busy, its streets crammed with vans and lorries, and raucous with rattling handcarts, shouts, whistling and cockney banter.

Another favourite area was Chelsea, especially dear to us because of all its arts associations. We liked its pubs and shops, the embankment and the Albert Bridge. We often wandered up and down the King's Road and particularly liked Green & Stone's the art suppliers. This shop had early associations with Augustus John and had been visited by almost every well-known artist, both past and present. Here we could examine papers and sketch pads, pastels and paints, inks and pens, brushes, pencils and easels of every shape and size. The range of goods was enormous. It was one of London's specialist shops, its quality unrivalled.

One memory is of when Ray took me to an old pub down the river, the Prospect of Whitby. I seem to remember that part of our journey involved an old part of the London underground tube system including an ancient creaking lift, or perhaps that was on another excursion.

A Pyramid Party, 1954

We spent a good deal of time visiting London Art Galleries. Although we were impressed by the National Gallery, our particular favourite was the National Portrait Gallery alongside.

I was especially fond of a large Elizabethan group portrait of a number of solemn elderly men sitting round a table at some sort of meeting. There was such a sense of immediacy about their portrayal that I felt myself actually standing there within their gaze.

The Royal Academy was a favourite too, elegant, welcoming and comfortable. Many years later Ray sold one of his paintings at their Summer Exhibition.

Before Tate Modern was built Tate Britain was the only Tate Gallery, at Millbank beside the river. Walking up its impressive steps to the entrance was always an occasion of excitement. I had been there first with my parents and we had enjoyed eating in their attractive restaurant with Rex Whistler murals on the wall.

There were a number of small private galleries in Mayfair. We didn't go inside these expensive establishments but enjoyed their frequently changed window displays.

Once, arriving early at Piccadilly Circus where we had arranged to meet before some gallery visiting, I stood on the pavement for some time. I was surprised when a rather over made-up older woman glared at me and then even more astonished when she drew nearer and hissed at me, 'Beginners on the other side if you **don't** mind!'. It took me a minute to realise what she meant. Fortunately Ray arrived at that point and we were able to make our laughing get-away.

I sometimes spent time with Anna, a friend who shared my hostel room. She introduced me to some of the places on our doorstep. Several times we went to church locally, and we went shopping in Swiss Cottage. My favourite place was a traditional tea shop in St John's Wood High Street.

We both liked the fact that there was a barracks nearby and sometimes we would see and hear a large number of beautiful bay horses trotting past on exercise.

On summer evening walks we found ourselves in quiet leafy streets of attractive houses where wealthy Edwardians had set up their mistresses in days gone by.

Anna had two brothers who were both doctors, as were her parents. Her family lived in Ireland outside Dublin. Her younger brother lived in London and we once went round to have supper. His attractive actress wife Aileen showed us how to make a delicious cheap spaghetti dish to feed a crowd. I used it frequently over the following years.

Hampton Court

As the weather grew warmer Ray and I met at the weekends to go further afield to Greenwich, Kew, Chiswick and Richmond. One Saturday, starting early, we walked from Kew beside the river all the way back down to Chelsea

Ray was particularly drawn to Hampton Court and we visited several times. Later I found out why. Very close to his parents' house at Ewell in Surrey was Nonsuch Park. It was where Henry VIII had built Nonsuch Palace, an elaborate and fantastically decorated building long since destroyed, all traces having disappeared.

From records it appear this palace was spectacular, not as large as some of Henry's many other palaces, but the last word in Tudor luxury. Apparently Henry did not have much opportunity to enjoy his grandiose new hunting lodge and only visited a few times before his death. The reign of his daughter Elizabeth was the heyday of Nonsuch.

As a very young boy Ray had been playing alone in the park one hot summer's day. Hearing clinking, jingling noises he looked up to see a troop of richly dressed men on horseback riding by, the vivid colours of their clothes bright against the greenery. Thrilled he rushed home to tell his mother who didn't pay much attention to this tale.

Many years later he saw oil paintings and book illustrations of Tudor hunting parties and recognised the extraordinary sight he had seen. From then on he became even more fascinated by Tudor history, particularly enjoying visits to Hampton Court. He studied Tudor history to the end of his life.

Nonsuch Palace

My special tree at Henley in Arden

Chapter 8 – Family visits and a new flat

Now that Ray and I were seriously involved we wanted to get to know each other's families. So one Saturday Ray took me to tea at his parents' home in Ewell. His family were more direct and blunt than mine but made me welcome from the start as we talked together with his mother and father, both Londoners.

Soon afterwards my parents came up to stay in Bailey's hotel in Kensington and we went to meet them there. My mother told me later that while they were waiting in the lounge a handsome but rather vacuous young man came in and my mother felt dismayed. When Ray and I turned up shortly afterwards she was pleased. 'Ray has so much more about him', she told me, 'and is much more interesting'. Relief all round.

After this I went several times to stay at Ewell for the weekend. I got to know Ray's older brother and his girlfriend and gradually became familiar with the area. Ray had grown up in Surrey since leaving Peckham at the age of four and had explored much of the county on foot and by bike and motorcycle over the years. He showed me some of his favourite haunts. Ewell itself was a very old village near Epsom, with a rich past history. Ray's home was in a 1930s style house but he knew stories about many of the impressive old houses in every type of architectural style.

Bourne Hall gatehouse, Ewell

We spent many hours in Nonsuch Park nearby and enjoyed visiting Epsom's shops and cinemas. As a child in Ewell Ray had been to the village school and had been a choir boy. In his early teens he had been a paper boy and a baker's boy.

For a while he had been to Epsom Art School where Birch, the principal, ruled benevolently over the students. One of Birch's friends was the famous artist Stanley Spencer. Stanley taught there occasionally, and was quite eccentric apparently, pushing his painting gear about on an old pram.

I also met Ray's friend Derek several times. In return for some caretaking duties he was able to live free in the lovely old Upper Mill, which straddled the small Hogsmill river. Once, as a boy, Ray had travelled quite a long way towards Kingston on a home-made raft on this river.

Downstream a little way from the mill was 'the Wilders' where local children played. The pre-Raphaelite painter Millais had used the river bank here, with its exquisite wild flowers, as background for his well-known painting of the drowning Ophelia.

An exciting part of these weekend visits was that Ray sometimes took me out on his motorbike. He and his brother had often taken part in motorbike trials. They had a particular friend nicknamed Spud who was a frequent winner of motorcycle events. We went once to watch him race.

In those days there were few health and safety rules. We didn't wear motorcycle helmets and I was happy to sit behind Ray, my arms round his waist. We would rocket off to the coast or enjoy a particular stretch of dual carriageway at the foot of Box Hill, well known for giving opportunities to do a 'ton' on its long straight stretch with little other traffic to create problems.

Before these weekend visits we would go across to 'The Compasses', a pub opposite Odhams, where many people from various magazines would go for a drink on Fridays, immediately after work. Then, taking my suitcase, we would go to Waterloo Station to catch the train to Ewell. I eagerly looked forward to visits there and enjoyed Ray's lively family.

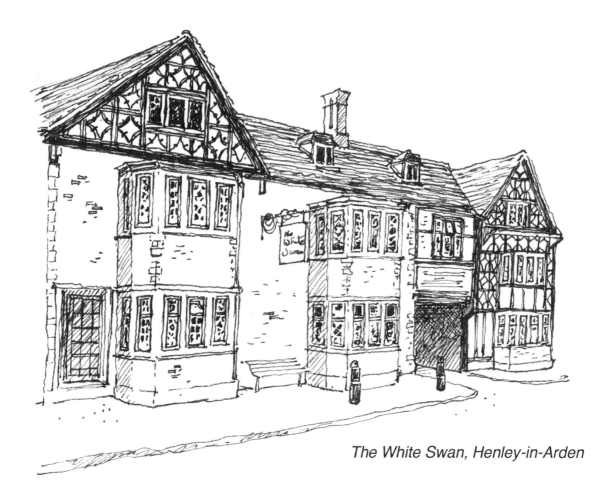

The White Swan, Henley-in-Arden

Then my mother and father asked me to invite Ray to come and stay in Hall Green for a week during the summer.

My parents had organised a family supper at the White Swan at Henley-in-Arden in Warwickshire. My mother's two brothers, my Uncle Ralph and Uncle Eric, came with their wives and my cousin Norma. It was discovered that Uncle Ralph, Norma's father, although dressed in a smart jacket, had come in his ancient gardening trousers which he had intended to change at the last moment but then forgot! It was a thoroughly happy time.

In Hall Green I showed Ray my version of 'the Wilders'. The place my friends and I had played was called 'the Dingles'. The little river Cole that ran through it and where we had fished for tiddlers was downstream from Sarehole Mill nearby. This mill featured in Tolkein's story of the Hobbit and was used as the setting for the place where Bilbo Baggins had started his great adventure. Tolkein had lived nearby as a child and had been impressed by the mill.

My father's friend Eric Thorneywork had a vintage Bugatti racing car and through him, my parents and I had often visited Prescott Hill climbing events out in the country towards Cheltenham. We took Ray to one of these events and all enjoyed it. I loved the tearing sounds of the car's exhausts as they revved up and the smell of the hot engine oil. We admired the glamorous vintage cars and their very individual drivers.

During the wartime I had lived with grandparents in Warwickshire villages and then later lived with my parents on a farm at Henley in Arden so we knew the area well.

Ray and I went on the bus from Hall Green and I took him to Buckley Green Farm where we had a picnic sitting in long grasses surrounded by butterflies. Then I took him up into my special tree, a large horse chestnut tree on the hillside. I had never invited anyone into this tree before and was very happy to have him there. I had certainly not imagined when I last sat there aged twelve that I would be sitting there later with my future husband.

After these family visits all our parents seemed happy that Ray and I had found each other. Back in London one of the older women on WOMAN magazine, seeing that Ray and I were now a couple, suggested that I should visit Dr Phillip Bloom in Harley Street to get fixed up with birth control. This was quite a daring suggestion for the time but I was very glad of this advice. In the days before the contraceptive pill was available Phillip Bloom and his wife were pioneers in this field of 'family planning' as it was then called. So many girls in those days lived in fear of becoming pregnant that I felt fortunate to have this opportunity.

* * * * *

Since the incident of the 'French dress' I was trying to dress in a more sophisticated way and had abandoned cardigans!

For some time I had been having my hair styled in a new way with a fringe. Sometimes I went to Richard Henry's well-known hair salon in Sloane Square. One Saturday morning, waiting for my appointment, I took out my sketchbook to make a quick drawing of an attractive client of his and her striking hairstyle. Richard Henry saw me drawing and came to look. After my hair had been done he took me aside to make me an offer. He told me that if I would go to work for him, sketching his clients so that they could have a drawing of themselves when they left, he would offer me more than I was currently being paid on WOMAN magazine. There was competition between top hairdressers and I suppose he thought this gimmick might give him an edge over his competitors. Startled, I thanked him and said I would let him know when I had thought it over.

Thank goodness I had Ray to discuss it with. I had been flattered by the offer and wondered whether to take it up. Ray didn't pour scorn on the idea, but just pointed out a few facts. My work on WOMAN offered much more variety than I would find sketching hair styles. As a member of the NUJ my job was protected. After a time, when the novelty wore off, Richard Henry might tire of this sketching scheme. Relieved by this common sense viewpoint I phoned Richard Henry to thank him for his offer but to tell him I was going to turn it down. He seemed surprised but took it in good part.

Richard Henry

* * * * *

Ray and I became officially engaged on my birthday in June and planned to get married as near as possible to Ray's birthday in September. We talked about where to go for our honeymoon and Ray asked if I had anywhere in mind. I knew immediately – Salcome in Devon. Salcome was a lovely seaside location in South Devon. I'd first stayed there with my parents when I was about six. Later Jean's parents had taken us there for a summer holiday. At the time we were rather awkward teenagers and looked enviously at the other sophisticated people staying there and wished we were more like them. To return with Ray on my honeymoon would be perfect!

With about three months to go before the wedding I fell in with the plans of two other girls at the John's Wood hostel. Jane, who shared a room with me and Pie, one of her friends, were well known to me and I liked them. We discussed it thoroughly. We all had boyfriends we wanted to see more of and were restless at the hostel. Between us we could afford a modest flat in roughly the same area of London. They would still have their occupational therapy classes to attend. We looked in the newspapers and chose about three flats to investigate. We found one we liked in West Hampstead. It was above a baker's shop fronting a small leafy square beside a church. It consisted of a kitchen and two rooms. One quite a large living room, had two beds where Pie and I could sleep. Jane had a smaller room to the back. I suppose it must have had a bathroom but I have no memory of it. Jane and Pie could get to St John's Wood on the tube and I could get down to Odhams in Holborn.

Flats were quite primitive in those days with very basic furnishings but it would suit us perfectly for a few months.

Our landlord was a handsome man. I think he may have been an actor. He had an older rather charming but faded wife. They seemed pleasant and we looked forward to moving in. Only when we had moved in did we find that they sometimes had the most tremendous rows. We could hear the landlord shouting and his wife crying although we had no idea what the rows were about. As these upsetting events were comparatively rare we decided to try to make the best of it.

We all got on well and enjoyed our new freedom. Pie and I had serious boyfriends with whom we spent most of our free time. Jane seemed to have plenty of people to go out with, but had not settled on one particular boyfriend.

Occasionally Pie and her boyfriend, and Ray and I made meals to share in the flat and all enjoyed each other's company. Because all of us girls were out often we only regularly shared some breakfast times together and parts of the weekend, especially Sunday evenings, as we prepared for each week ahead. I remember a sunny summer with carefree days.

One day we arrived back at the flat to find a bowl of filthy water on our kitchen table and an angry note from our landlord. We were shocked to find that he had washed our kitchen floor and that the filthy water was the result. Busy working or studying or out with our boyfriends, all but the most rudimentary housework hadn't even crossed our minds. We did our own washing and ironing and prepared very basic meals with food we bought ourselves. We kept our rooms tidy and that was about it. Used to our own homes or the hostel where housework had not been required of us we were all three of us completely undomesticated so felt rather ashamed about our neglect of basic chores.

After this we made spasmodic attempts to keep the flat clean, but didn't change our mindset much! Each week we paid our rent to the landlord on Saturday morning. Actually we usually paid his wife, but before one particular weekend she had told us she would be away for a week.

On the Saturday morning I offered to take our money upstairs to the landlord's flat on the top floor. I knocked at his door with the money ready. He turned away to fetch his cash box and the door, which he had been holding partially closed, swung silently open. I saw a beautiful young man asleep on their sofa. The landlord turned round and realised what I had seen. A level look passed between us – no words were spoken. My look conveyed the message that I would make no mention of this incident, but that I would expect no more nagging about our housekeeping, or lack of it. His look conveyed that as I now had the upper hand he would comply with my expectations.

I was taking advantage of the fact that, in 1955, homosexuality was illegal, but didn't feel too bad about my mild blackmail because I was not going to mention this to anyone else. Now I realised what the rows had been about and felt sorry for the landlady. I later found out that in those days gay men would sometimes marry unsuspecting women to give themselves 'cover'. No wonder they were unhappy together. Thank goodness in our more enlightened times gay people can live openly together with dignity and without censure. From then on I made rather more effort with the housekeeping and the landlord regarded me warily with tenuous approval. Life was providing a steep learning curve.

* * * * *

Jane, Pie and I decided to throw a party. As we couldn't spend much, it was to be a bottle party where every guest brought a bottle with them. We provided plentiful snacks and hired glasses. I invited Ray and his friend Tony who brought a girlfriend. Pie invited her boyfriend and one or two others. Jane, who was more part of the local scene than we were, invited some of the members of Hampstead Cricket Club. They, in turn, told other members of the cricket club who turned up unexpectedly with their girlfriends. To our slight alarm the flat was soon packed with people. However, everyone was very pleasant and jolly and we looked forward to a good evening. As a precaution we had chosen a Saturday evening when we knew the landlord was to be away. We had invited the landlady to the party. Plied with drinks and made much of she seemed happy enough, but after some time retired upstairs.

By this time dancing to our record player had begun. It was a glorious summer evening and all our windows were wide open. The noise of the party was considerable. Ray and I decided to go across to the other side of the square to assess the noise, bearing in mind the reaction of the neighbours. Through the trees we saw a police car draw up and stop below the lighted windows. Someone must have complained already! Looking up the police could see young people dancing wildly but it all seemed good natured – no fights or rows, just people enjoying themselves. They drove off without even getting out of the police car!

Ray and I were married in West Hampstead in 1955

Chapter 9 – Getting married

Ray and I began to make wedding preparations. We had already booked a week at Tides Reach, our chosen hotel in Salcombe. We went to a smart cake shop in Regent Street and ordered our wedding cake to be topped with a decorative artist's palette and brushes made of icing sugar. My parents booked Bailey's hotel in South Kensington for our wedding reception and Ray and I went along to discuss menus and arrangements with the manager.

I began organising my wedding outfit. In VOGUE magazine I had just recently seen a lovely wedding picture of a young model in a short wedding outfit – not the traditional long white wedding dress and decided this is what I would like.

I knew a very pleasant older woman who came into WOMAN magazine to make clothes for our photographic fashion models. Her name was Gwen Rushman. She had invited Jane and I to stay with her one weekend and I had painted her beautiful garden for her. I asked her if she could recommend a dressmaker. She immediately offered to make my wedding dress herself at no charge as a gift. I was overwhelmed by the kind and generous offer. I chose a beautiful fabric, a slightly stiff silk grosgrain in a silvery green colour. Then I saw a fabulous hat in a boutique in Baker Street. It was made of silk, shading from the palest pink to deep rose and shaped into three roses, very light and pretty. Finally I found some long kid gloves in palest pink at Gallerie Lafayette where I had bought my French dress.

Ray and I had been making enquiries about a flat to rent for ourselves but did not particularly like any of those we had seen. As usual my father turned out to be a wonderful help. He had a business friend who worked in London and had heard of a flat falling vacant in Edgware, and so we arranged a viewing. It was just right ... large and in good repair on the top floor of a 30s style block, one of three at the entrance to leafy Canon's Drive. Many of the residents were Jewish, friendly and pleasant. We paid a deposit and moved in our very few pieces of furniture with the welcome help of Ray's brother. Edgware was at the end of the Bakerloo tube line, which we could use to get down to Odhams each day.

Next we needed to meet a local vicar to make our wedding arrangements. We walked up the hill to the smart Hampstead Church well known for society weddings. We had rung to make an appointment to see the vicar. As we approached his house on the Saturday morning he came out and chatted to us on the pavement. He showed us his car at the kerb and asked Ray if he could change a tyre for him. I could see that Ray was astonished at the request but complied in the hope that this might influence the vicar favourably towards us. When the job was completed the vicar told us that as we lived in West Hampstead we should approach a church in that area. His church was unavailable for us!

The vicar we approached in West Hampstead at the church only a hundred yards or so from our flat, could not have been more different. He was sincere, serious and welcoming. We went to him for talks before the wedding and both warmed to him and were very pleased he would be marrying us.

* * * * *

A week or so before the wedding there was a big upheaval at Odhams which affected Ray. Management had decided that most of the staff working on PICTUREGOER magazine were to move to work on ILLUSTRATED. This left vacancies at PICTUREGOER and Ray was offered the job of Art Editor. This was an exciting promotion. Ray, at 25, would be one of the youngest art editors on the magazine scene. So not only was he to have a new home and a new wife, but a new job too! We were delighted.

* * * * *

We were to be married on Saturday 17 September. My parents drove up to London the day before, bringing my grandfather and my childhood friend Margaret. My uncles, aunts and cousin made their own way. Ann and Jean were coming and Ann was to be my bridesmaid. That day was dark with heavy rain all day. Ann stayed overnight with me and when we opened the curtains next day we were delighted to find blue skies and golden sunshine – a glorious September day. At mid-morning Ann went to join my family and Ray's family at the church. My father came to collect me and we walked over together, full of joy. I remember a tremendously happy day. It was quite a small wedding, just our immediate family and friends. Pat McNeil, who had helped me since I first arrived on WOMAN was there, and Ray's friend Tony was his best man.

One slight hitch was the fact that my father, who was the photographer in the family, was so happy and excited by the whole event that although he took masses of colour photographs, he found later that he had forgotten to put any film in his camera! Fortunately a friend of Rays was a professional photographer and he had made a black and white cine film for us. We used this later to make stills of the wedding for ourselves friends and family.

After our wedding lunch and reception at Baileys, we said fond farewells and caught the train to Devon. We arrived at the lovely comfortable hotel in the dark, waking next morning to the glorious views from South Sands Bay at Salcombe. We had an idyllic honeymoon with perfect weather, and went swimming, cliff climbing, walking and exploring. An elderly French waiter at the hotel looked after us benevolently and was determined to feed us up!

Some evenings after dinner we would walk into Salcombe itself to an old waterside inn, before walking back later under glittering September stars. As we got ready to leave we vowed to come back and one day we did, on our fortieth wedding anniversary!

Picturegoer was a popular film magazine of the time

The boathouse beside Tides Reach hotel, Salcombe

By then the hotel had been greatly enlarged and updated but still retained its wonderful position and atmosphere.

* * * * *

Shortly after our return to London and our new flat in Edgware, hard reality set in! Previously I had spent most of my evenings and weekends going out with Ray or seeing friends. Any clothes washing, cooking or cleaning had been spasmodic. Now, for the first time in my life, I was responsible for running a home. This involved serious amounts of shopping, cooking, washing and ironing, mending and cleaning. I wanted to do it well, remembering the warm, comfortable and attractive homes that my mother had always created, but was taken aback by the amount of sheer hard work involved. This work also had to be accomplished while working full time from Monday to Friday at Odhams.

After some rather erratic beginnings, struggles and mistakes, I became a fairly competent housewife after about six months. Throughout this period Ray worked alongside me and helped me to organise my jobs and responsibilities. Once, seeing me looking rather mulish over some future task, he said. 'Gill, I'm not trying to ask you to work for the sake of it. It's just that if we can do our jobs quickly this gives us so much time over to enjoy ourselves!'

This outlook was very different from my own, where I did my favourite jobs first and tried to forget about some of the most boring ones. Reluctantly I could see the advantages in Ray's point of view and changed my ideas and became more proficient. I suppose one point in my favour domestically – perhaps the only one! – was that I had always liked cooking and really enjoyed preparing meals. This certainly helped.

At this period it was generally assumed that wives would do most of the domestic work in the home, even though their working hours might be as long as their husbands. Luckily for me Ray was too fair-minded to agree with this. He never sat about reading the paper while I did housework as some young husbands did. During these early months he redecorated the flat throughout, which was no small undertaking. The flat had been in good order when we moved in, but just not to our taste. The couple who lived there before us had favoured fitted carpets, net curtains and predominant shades of cream, fawn and pink, not our style at all.

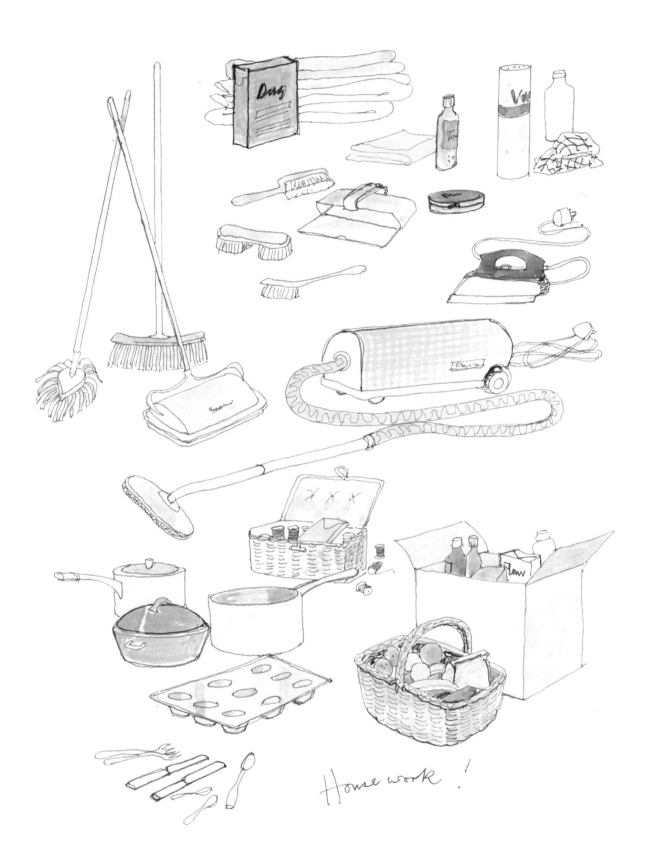

Housework !

Many young people at that time were moving towards brighter colours and had very decided tastes in new sharper furnishings. Ray made our smallest bedroom into a workshop with his carpentry bench from home and newly bought decorating equipment. He repainted every surface and made pieces of furniture and built-in-units. We had a long corridor with doors opening off it. He painted each door a different glossy colour and replaced old door handles with wooden door knobs painted in contrasting colours.

I benefitted from his energy and enthusiasm and my friends and family were surprised and impressed. This period was the beginning of a huge 'Do it Yourself' boom which hit decorating at this time.

We had very little furniture: a cooker, kitchen stools and table, two single beds from Ray's home pushed together to make a double bed, and some dining room chairs that had belonged to an elderly aunt of Rays. Uncle Ralph had given us a wedding cheque for fifty pounds with which we bought two supremely comfortable Parker Knoll wing chairs at twenty five pounds each. The price of the equivalent chairs today would be many hundreds of pounds. Gradually we bought curtains, carpets, rugs, pieces of furniture and kitchen equipment. This was the norm then for many young couples starting married life together – almost always in flats rather than houses. Very few had fully kitted out homes to start with. This was before the days of hire purchase and few paid for goods by instalments.

It was Ray's idea to do jobs every evening so that most of the weekends were free. We also had Wednesday evenings off every week and went to local cinemas. We travelled together down to Odhams on the tube each day and despite all our involvement with domestic issues and changes, were extremely happy together.

We enjoyed having friends and family to the flat. Once my father came to stay for a few days visiting the Motor Show in Earl's Court. He and Ray both enjoyed Marx Brothers films so we took him one evening to a Marx Brothers film at an old fashioned little cinema in Baker Street. As we bought our tickets we were asked if we would like to order tea for the interval. Then at the interval itself a posse of elderly ladies appeared with our trays. We looked at each other in amazement – it seemed too good to be true.

We found useful shops locally in Edgware. There was a dusty antiques shop in an old half-timbered building where we picked up special treasures and a good old fashioned butchers and grocers side by side. At the grocers, run by an elderly man and his two sisters, we once bought a shabby box of pre-war Christmas crackers with splendid quality gifts inside.

There was also a lively record shop where we often dropped in on Saturdays. Ray was building up his eclectic record collection. We liked the big bands of Duke Ellington, Glen Miller and Benny Goodman, jazz and classical music. Ray enjoyed English plain song and Early English Music, but opportunities to hear these were few and far between.

We often listened to our records and music on the radio. I remember when Bill Hayley and the Comets released Rock Around the Clock – a fresh, invigorating sound. It was impossible to listen to it and keep still.

There was a very useful corner shop right opposite the flats where we went frequently. Fish fingers had just been invented and were available there – very useful for a simple meal in a hurry! I remembered some of the meals my mother had shown me and found WOMAN recipes a great help as I developed my cooking repertoire. The recipes were so clearly and simply set out that you couldn't go wrong if you followed them carefully. Once I improvised with disappointing results. I used a recipe from WOMAN for a traditional Christmas cake. Because I didn't want a large one I used a quarter of all the ingredients thinking that this would make a small cake. Unfortunately, because I used a large tin, this resulted in a cooked layer of ingredients about an inch high. I was mortified. Ray thought it tasted fine so on his suggestion I cut it into small cubes, dusted them in icing sugar and presented them as Christmas sweetmeats. They were very popular. A typical example of Ray's lateral thinking and making the best of things.

Our Edgware flat

Chapter 10 – Living in Edgware

One of the best things about our new flat was that the windows, in the 1930s style bay in the living room, opened onto tree tops near the entrance to Canons Drive. We began to explore.

We discovered that Canons Drive had originally been the driveway to an important house, set in parkland. In the early 18th century the Duke of Chandos had lived here and had invited many important people of the day to visit. Reputedly, when Handel came he had played the organ in the nearby family church. More recently, after the original house was demolished and a second house built, this was purchased in 1929 by the North London Collegiate School run by the legendary Miss Buss and Miss Beale. At the time we lived in Edgware, a large number of Jewish people lived there, some of them in the expensive houses, which now lined Canons Drive. They were not unfriendly to us but were very involved with their own close family and social ties.

Ray and I continued to travel down to central London on the tube every day to work on our respective magazines. Ray was enjoying his new job on PICTUREGOER. He was able to give free reign to his own creative ideas, and was good at handling his colleagues – a necessary skill, as he was younger than most of the staff. I was excited to learn that one day he met Frank Sinatra who was in London for some film publicity.

We met friends, had visitors to our flat and continued our cinema visits in town. A favourite restaurant on evenings out was Bianchi's Italian restaurant in Soho. Ray had been going there for some years and knew the people who ran it and we both loved its old-fashioned interior and delicious food.

Most of my colleagues on WOMAN took a keen interest in other magazines and the work of other journalists. We often read the 'agony aunt' articles written by Marjorie Proops and were pleased that she made an amusing speech to open a Journalists Ball held at the Festival Hall, which we attended. Another favourite woman writer was Katherine Whitehorn who was rather more upmarket.

* * * * *

In contrast to this pleasant way of life, two disturbing events worried us towards the end of 1956. One morning I arrived at the WOMAN offices to find Beata crying and distraught. She was a writer on the magazine, a sophisticated older woman and we knew her well. She was Hungarian and her family lived in Hungary. She had just heard on the radio that Soviet tanks were rolling into Hungary and was desperately fearful for her relations. Hungary was under Soviet domination and when students in Budapest challenged the Stalinist First Secretary, the State Secret Police fired on the students. The Hungarian people rose in fury. Bitter fighting broke out. Calls came through on the radio to other countries: 'Help us! Help us!' At first my friends and I were horrified that our government and the rest of Europe failed to respond. Then we realised that, although wanting to help, no one was prepared to take on the Russians and start another conflict after the terrible experiences of the recent world war. 10,000 people died in Budapest alone. These statistics shook the West, but still the Hungarians were left without help. Brutal tactics put down the Hungarian uprising in barely four weeks.

The second event following hot on the heels of this first disaster was known as the Suez Crisis. President Nasser of Egypt nationalised the Suez Canal, long important to the British during the running of its Empire. In response the British Conservative government launched what was later described as 'one of the most inept and inexcusable invasions of all time', aided by French and Israeli troops.

After leaving the army Ray had become a part-time member of the territorial army. Like many other 'territorials' he feared he might be called up if our invasion of the Canal Zone continued. After a brief spell of fighting the UN and the USA put pressure on the French and British to withdraw, and UN peacekeeping troops moved in.

Ray and I were relieved that he would not have to leave to fight. Many people in Britain had been against the invasion. There had been other serious conflicts during the fifties but we felt most concerned about the Hungarian uprising and the Suez crisis because they involved us more directly.

By far the deepest fear in those days was the threat of the Atom Bomb. However, because the threat was so immense, and the ways some people were preparing for it by stockpiling food and building individual shelters was so pathetically inadequate, we somehow put it out of our minds and refused to live in perpetual fear. Many people went on protest marches.

Later, during the sixties, we became worried about the almost casual use of nuclear testing. I joined a group called 'Voice of Women', conceived and developed by its founder Judith Cook, and we worked to get nuclear testing banned. After some time, and pressure from many powerful groups and many sides this took place and we felt deep relief.

Another Odhams party

After the Suez crisis Ray suggested that if we wanted to start a family it would be a good idea to start now so that we would be young parents. I agreed, we stopped using birth control and I became pregnant almost immediately. I was excited, but also a bit daunted by the development.

During this time we met friends, and saw more of Ray's friend Tony. At weekends we frequently went to stay with Ray's parents at Ewell. My parents moved from Hall Green in Birmingham to the pretty village of Whitchurch in Buckinghamshire so my father would collect us in the car and we had weekends with my parents too. These weekends away from housework and chores undoubtedly made life easier even apart from the great pleasure of seeing our families.

* * * * *

Because I would leave Odhams six weeks before the birth of our baby, we started thinking about freelance artwork I would be able to do at home. Ray had asked me if I wanted to have an au pair to look after the baby, while I continued to work, but I definitely did not want to share our life with an au pair and wanted to look after my baby myself.

One of the freelance jobs that turned up sounded very interesting. The British Medical Association were bringing out a series of booklets to be sold in every chemist, offering information and advice on a wide range of subjects. They were looking for more illustrators for the series. I went to the prestigious BMA and was asked to illustrate a booklet about the Alexander Technique which helped correct bad posture.

Posture problems
illustration

I was asked to visit Charles Neil, the well-known practitioner and author of this booklet, who lived in Holland Park. I remember a charming man who explained clearly what he wanted and offered me a delicious vegetarian lunch to share with him and his staff. I began work at once, making a series of black and white illustrations. For example, the one illustrated here, shows a group of five people, all with incorrect posture, that would be treated and helped by the Alexander Technique. I was making these drawings in the six weeks before my baby was due after I had left Odhams.

My clever Jewish doctor had been determined to book me in to University College Hospital for my` maternity care. Ray and I and our families were getting excited by now. When my labour pains started very early one morning Ray came down to the hospital with me in an ambulance before going on to work. Our son Mark was born at 12 o'clock, later that morning, and I was given a phone so that I could ring Ray and tell him that he had a son!

As was the custom in those days I then stayed in hospital with all the other new mothers for a fortnight. Our time was spent almost entirely in bed in a large sunny ward. We were treated very well and the whole thing was free on the NHS. It's really only in retrospect that I realise how very lucky we were. After a pleasant time in hospital with many visits from Ray, friends and family, it was time to go home in early September 1957.

Once again, hard reality set in. After the period in hospital when we were only presented with our clean, cared for babies when it was time for us to feed them, or to have them beside us in their cribs for a short time each day – suddenly we were responsible for them 24 hours a day.

My mother came with Ray to collect me from the hospital in a taxi and then she stayed for a week doing all the cooking and generally being a wonderful help. Husbands had no paternity leave then so soon I was left on my own to care for the baby. I had no previous experience of handling babies and found it another steep learning curve. The plus side was that Ray and I were thrilled with our new son and I had Ray's help and company every evening and during the weekends.

Most new mothers in those days slavishly followed the guidance set out in a popular baby book by 'Doctor Spock' until they gradually gained confidence. Eventually it all became easier. How I would love to have had my mother living nearby. I had a particular friend, Stella, who lived on the other side of Edgware within walking distance. We had met at University College Hospital and found we were near neighbours. Stella's baby, born at the same time as Mark, was her second daughter. We would push prams to each other's houses. Some of the young Jewish mothers were friendly but their lifestyles and priorities were so different from mine that we had very little in common – it was a bit like living abroad.

Kenneth Haigh, actor, and John Osborne, playwright

As I began to do more freelance and was earning again I decided to spend some of the money on employing a cleaner for a couple of hours a week. Mrs Berry who answered my advertisement, was a large rather gruff lady who turned out to have a heart of gold. I grew very fond of her as she told me about her family and she grew to know Mark. Soon she offered to babysit Mark for us, so we could continue our outings to the local cinemas. We really appreciated her help and her obvious fondness for our son.

* * * * *

During this period there was a significant social change. People began to be assessed by their talents and achievements rather than by their class, education and background.

John Osbourne's play, Look Back in Anger, which premiered at the Royal Court Theatre in 1957, gave voice to this change in challenging dramatic form. Michael Billington, writing in the Guardian of Osbourne's play, commented that it 'tackled sex, class, religion, politics, the press and the sense of a country stifled by an official establishment culture'. The play was a vivid outpouring of resentment against the established social scene. Alan Sillitoe wrote 'British Theatre can never be the same again'. It was not only the theatre that changed. Writers, photographers, film-makers, actors and artists began to give expression to this new liberation from the establishment.

Freelance illustration

David Bailey, the photographer, and Michael Caine, the actor, typified those who benefitted from new opportunities for talented newcomers in every field. Ray said 'Look Back in Anger' mirrored some of his own experiences and frustrations. I found it exaggeratedly vituperative, but I had not been patronised or held back like Ray in his younger days.

As we discussed his earlier days he told me of an incident that absolutely delighted me. One lunchtime at Odhams a new member of the management staff came across him in the art studio. 'Are you doing anything this lunchtime Thomas? No? then I'll take you out to lunch – a decent lunch!' Implying that this would be a great treat for Ray, who had probably never had such a thing. He took Ray to the Wig and Pen Club opposite the Law Courts and ushered him inside. A waiter came hurrying up, and the manager looked gratified. He was rather less pleased when the waiter turned to Ray and enquired, 'Your usual table Mr Thomas?'

'Look Back in Anger' was later made into a film with Richard Burton playing Jimmy Porter in the lead, a perfect choice for the part. Long afterwards reading John Osbourne's autobiography Ray realised that he and Osbourne had both been at Ewell Boy's School for a while and had shared an enterprise selling second hand comics!

Now that I had left Odhams I was happy with my lively baby in our Edgware flat, especially as I had a variety of freelance art opportunities to explore. Ray carried work up and down to London for me and, if I needed to meet the people who were commissioning me, he would look after Mark while I went up to London on Saturday mornings. I did illustrations for WOMAN, WOMAN'S REALM, WOMAN SENSE and another booklet for the BMA. I also remember some work to illustrate a book written about adoption, and one or two other magazines.

Mrs Berry now offered to look after Mark sometimes during the day. I remember sitting in the hairdressers one morning and seeing her passing with Mark's pushchair as they went to feed the ducks on the large pond not far from the entrance to Canon's Drive. They were chatting happily away together. Sometimes she took him home to her house. Mr Berry was a bus driver who worked shifts and was sometimes at home too. Mark told me they had rabbits in a hutch in their garden and he would go with Mr Berry to feed them before they sat down at the kitchen table for drinks of milk and tea respectively.

Ray told me about his colleagues on PICTUREGOER. He liked the humour of Arthur Gould, his Editor, and admired Margaret Hinxman, the well-known film reviewer. Sometimes Ray went to small private morning viewings of much anticipated films. They were advanced viewings for the critics. Once I went with him, I think my mother must have been babysitting. It was exciting.

Between us, by now, we knew quite a large number of Odham's staff and we enjoyed the variety of people we had worked alongside.

A large part of our life in London together had been our pleasure eating out in a variety of small restaurants: Hungarian, Greek, Indian, German, Italian and French.

Our absolute favourite was still Bianchi's Italian restaurant in Frith Street. The food in this Soho restaurant was authentic, simple and perfect. Sometimes Elena Salvoni was present. She was a small vibrant woman of immense warmth who presided over the restaurant with authority and charm. Bianchi's was always popular with writers, artists, actors and musicians. It was part of the Soho post-war rebirth that took place.

Later, in the 60s, Ronnie Scott's Jazz Club relocated opposite the restaurant and it was a particular pleasure to sit upstairs in Bianchi's on a warm summer's evening with the strains of jazz music floating across the narrow street through the wide open windows.

From the time of my teenage visits to London in the early fifties right up to the end of the decade I had found London to be full of surprises and contrasts.

No matter how grand and imposing some of its official buildings might be there was always the human element: a modest little eating place nearby and busy activity with messenger boys and delivery vans.

Impressive formal town houses had tiny mews cottages tucked between them. Every district had its own very distinctive character and attributes, its own life and energy. The variety and interest of this great city was never-ending.

Aftermath

Finally the decade was drawing to a close. Towards the end of the 50s we started another baby and began serious searches for a new home. We wanted to bring up our children in the country. We were happy to find a little house in Cove in Hampshire. This would mean commuting on the steam train the thirty miles to London each day for Ray. Our second son Matthew was born in 1960 to family rejoicing, bringing the start of a new way of life for us and closer ties with our parents.

Ray and I looked back at the fifties in London with gratitude – it had been a time of opportunities for both of us. At the beginning of the decade we had both been general artists in advertising studios. By the end Ray was an experienced art editor and I was an accepted illustrator.

The sixties and the decades that followed brought increasing affluence and stability but we appreciated the fifties for shifts in social expectations and the start of fresh possibilities after the long aftermath of the Second World War. London had lived up to all my expectations.

Mark and Matthew growing up in Hampshire

Acknowledgements

Thanks to my family for their continual enthusiasm for this project.

Thank you to my publisher, Matt Trollope.

Thank you to my friend Jo Rolfe for her careful proof-reading.

Thank you to Sharon Alward and Marina Marriott at Sharward Services Ltd for their patience and skill.

Thank you for the V&A pictorial archive for permission to use the photograph of Barbara Goalen.

Thank you to Robert Opie from the Museum Of Brands, Packaging & Advertising for permission to use the selection of magazine covers on pages 36 and 75.

Thank you to the painter Hugh Webster and the Tuesday Group at his Felixstowe Ferry Boatshed studio for their continuous encouragement.

I would be happy to remunerate any person who can prove ownership of the copyright of the Francis Marshall illustrations I have included, as I could not discover them.

Born in 1933, Gill trained initially at Birmingham College of Art in the early fifties and then worked as an illustrator in advertising in Birmingham and in publishing in London.

She married the artist Ray Thomas in 1955 and has two sons.

After a lifetime spent in education she became an advisory teacher for Hampshire County Council and taught for a time at Reading University.

During her retirement in Suffolk Gill studied for her Fine Art degree and gained her BA Hons at Suffolk University in 2008.

She continues to work as an illustrator and painter.

Gill's first book:

My Warwickshire Wartime
1939 - 1945

At the outset of World War II many children were evacuated from the big cities into the countryside to avoid the threat of bombing. Gill was lucky to leave Birmingham to stay with her Granny Emett who lived in the small Warwickshire village of Halford.

What follows is a sharply observed account; a child's eye view of the wartime years in rural England, including detailed, poignant and sometimes hilarious memories of her life as a boarder at the Croft School, Stratford on Avon, throughout the war.

Gill's Uncle was the famous wartime cartoonist, Rowland Emett of Punch magazine, and some of his unique drawings add to the lavish illustrations of this evocative book.

Made in the USA
Columbia, SC
11 January 2018